SUPERSTARS
of
PRO FOOTBALL

DONOVAN McNABB

Michael Chatlien

Mason Crest Publishers

Produced by OTTN Publishing in association with
21st Century Publishing and Communications, Inc.

MASON CREST PUBLISHERS INC.
370 Reed Road
Broomall, Pennsylvania 19008
(866) MCP-BOOK (toll free)
www.masoncrest.com

Printed in the United States of America.

First Printing

9 8 7 6 5 4 3 2 1

Library of Congress Cataloging-in-Publication Data

Chatlien, Michael.
   Donovan McNabb / Michael Chatlien.
     p. cm. — (Superstars of pro football)
   Includes index.
ISBN 978-1-4222-0559-4 (hardcover) — ISBN 978-1-4222-0829-8 (pbk.)
   1. McNabb, Donovan—Juvenile literature. 2. Football players—United States—
Biography—Juvenile literature. 3. Quarterbacks (Football)—United States—
Biography—Juvenile literature. I. Title.
GV939.M38C53 2008
796.332092—dc22
[B]   2008024183

Publisher's note:
All quotations in this book come from original sources, and contain the spelling
and grammatical inconsistencies of the original text.

◀◀ CROSS-CURRENTS ▶▶

In the ebb and flow of the currents of life we are each influenced
by many people, places, and events that we directly experience or
have learned about. Throughout the chapters of this book you will
come across **CROSS-CURRENTS** reference bubbles. These bubbles
direct you to a **CROSS-CURRENTS** section in the back of the
book that contains fascinating and informative sidebars
and related pictures. Go on. ▶▶

◀◀CONTENTS▶▶

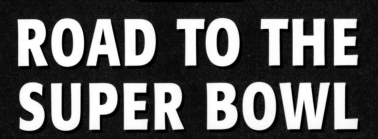

ROAD TO THE SUPER BOWL

O n January 23, 2005, the weather conditions in Philadelphia were rough for a football game. The temperature was -5° Fahrenheit (-21° Celsius), and winds gusted up to 26 miles per hour. It was so cold that steam rose off a player's head when he pulled off his helmet. Donovan McNabb and the Philadelphia Eagles, however, were familiar with tough conditions.

Winning the Championship

For each of the past three years, the Eagles had reached the **National Football Conference (NFC)** championship game, only to be defeated. In 2005, their fourth straight year playing for

Philadelphia Eagles quarterback Donovan McNabb holds up the George Halas Trophy, January 23, 2005. The Eagles had won the trophy—and earned a trip to Super Bowl XXIX—by defeating the Atlanta Falcons, 27-10, in the NFC Championship game.

CROSS-CURRENTS

Read "Falcons Quarterback Michael Vick" to learn more about the player the Eagles had to stop to win the NFC Championship. Go to page 46. ▶▶

the NFC title, the Eagles faced the Atlanta Falcons and their hotshot quarterback Michael Vick. The pressure to win was intense.

Despite this pressure, Donovan McNabb, the quarterback for the Eagles, was confident. He was so confident, in fact, that he told head coach Andy Reid he wanted to run the "Fox 2 Double Short Comeback" as the first play of the game.

This short passing play had failed miserably in the Eagles' playoff game against the Minnesota Vikings. Reid

Donovan races away from Falcons defensive linemen Antwan Lake (left) and Brady Smith for a six-yard pickup during the second quarter of the NFC Championship game. Throughout the game, Donovan kept the Falcons' defense off balance, running for 32 yards and passing for 180, including two touchdowns.

was surprised but pleased that McNabb had chosen this play. The decision showed guts. Reid called the "Fox Comeback" as the game's first play, and Donovan and the offense **executed** it perfectly. They completed a 13-yard pass. Later Donovan commented:

> **"It set the tempo. It showed we weren't going to sit back and play conservative in this weather."**

The Eagles continued to set the tempo, scoring a touchdown in the first quarter on their second drive. After a long gain by running back Brian Westbrook and a 21-yard pass from Donovan to tight end L.J. Smith, running back Dorsey Levens plunged into the end zone from four yards out. A second-quarter drive produced another touchdown. During that drive, Donovan connected on three passes, including a 45-yard strike to wide receiver Greg Lewis and a 3-yard touchdown toss to tight end Chad Lewis.

Meanwhile, the Eagles' defense was containing Michael Vick. Vick was a **scrambling** quarterback. He often gained more yards running, or rushing, the football than he did passing it. During this game, however, Vick gained only 26 yards rushing.

At halftime, the score was 14-10 in favor of the Eagles. In the second half, Philadelphia added two field goals and a touchdown (on another Donovan McNabb to Chad Lewis connection) to secure a 27-10 win.

Fans in the stadium waved towels, cried, and hugged each other. The Eagles were on their way to the Super Bowl! As the players went to the locker room, they shouted, "One more! One more!" In a postgame interview, an **ecstatic** Donovan said:

> **"I think . . . you've seen a team that just continued to stay loose and stayed focused on the task at hand, and our task at hand was to put ourselves in position to go to the Super Bowl and possibly win it."**

Path to the Playoffs

How did this magical season happen? The 2004 season actually started with some doubts. The main question came with the signing of Terrell Owens (T.O.), a wide receiver known to make big plays.

Some people wondered if T.O. could get along with Donovan. Donovan was known as a team player, but T.O. had the reputation of being a troublemaker who could upset a team's chemistry. The two stars, however, seemed to hit it off from the beginning.

In the first game of the year, Owens was Donovan's go-to guy. Donovan completed eight passes for 68 yards to T.O. Three of those passes were for touchdowns. The Eagles went on to defeat the New York Giants, 31-17.

The chemistry between Donovan and Owens continued to thrive as the Eagles won their first seven games of the year. This streak included a dramatic overtime win over the Cleveland Browns on October 24. The Browns tried to stop Owens by **double-teaming** him, so Donovan just spread the ball around to other receivers. Donovan ended up completing 28 of 43 passes for 376 yards and four touchdowns.

Later in the season, on December 19, the Eagles had a come-from-behind victory against the Dallas Cowboys. In this game, Donovan led a drive late in the fourth quarter for a touchdown, which gave the Eagles a 12-7 win. The team finished the regular season with 13 wins and three losses.

In the first game of the playoffs, the Eagles were without T.O., who had injured his ankle. Even so, they smothered the Vikings 27-14. The Eagles then defeated the Falcons in the NFC Championship game. This win set the stage for a Super Bowl matchup with the tough New England Patriots. The Patriots had won two Super Bowls in the previous three years. Leading up to the big game, however, the Eagles received encouraging news—T.O. would be able to play.

CROSS-CURRENTS

To learn more about the history of the NFL's annual championship game, check out "The Super Bowl." Go to page 47. ▶▶

Super Bowl XXXIX

Super Bowl XXXIX was tightly fought. By the third quarter, the score was tied 14-14. Then the Patriots scored a touchdown and a field goal, giving them 10 more points.

Donovan tried to get his team back into the game. The Eagles scored a touchdown with 1 minute and 48 seconds left, but it was too little, too late. The Patriots won, 24-21.

An enthusiastic Donovan McNabb answers a reporter's question at a media event before Super Bowl XXXIX. Donovan and the Eagles went into the big game with great confidence, but they fell a little short, losing to the New England Patriots by three points.

Donovan threw for 357 yards and three touchdowns, but it wasn't enough. Despite the crushing loss, Donovan remained positive in his post-game comments:

"I'm going to keep my head up high, not low. It's still a successful year, definitely. All the challenges we faced, people talking about what we weren't going to be able to do. . . . We did a lot."

Donovan's positive attitude in the face of defeat was nothing new. It had served him well during his childhood and early career.

SPORTS FAN TO SPORTS STAR

Donovan McNabb was born on November 25, 1976, on Chicago's South Side. Donovan's father, Sam, worked as an electrical engineer. His mother, Wilma, was a nurse. Despite working long hours, Donovan's parents spent plenty of quality time with their two children. Wilma listened to any secrets they wanted to share, and Sam gave them lots of good advice.

Growing Up

The McNabb family lived in a tough Chicago neighborhood. Donovan's parents were worried about their children. When

The quarterback (right) was joined by his family at a 2006 event sponsored by the Donovan McNabb Foundation, which focuses on helping people with diabetes. From left: Donovan's older brother, Sean; his mother, Wilma; and his father, Sam.

Donovan was eight, he and his family moved to a safer neighborhood in Dolton, Illinois.

Dolton, a Chicago suburb, had a mostly white population. Most people there welcomed the McNabbs, who were African American. However, soon after the family arrived, **vandals** wrecked their home. The family was very upset.

From an early age, Donovan was a big sports fan. He tore out magazine photos of sports stars and papered his bedroom wall with them. His older brother, Sean, was considered the athlete in the family, though. For a while, Donovan managed Sean's basketball team.

CROSS-CURRENTS

To learn about Donovan McNabb's work with one charitable organization, read "Donovan's Fight Against Diabetes." Go to page 48. ▶▶

At age 11, Donovan watched African-American quarterback Doug Williams play in the Super Bowl. Williams was the first black quarterback to play in this game. Soon, Donovan told his mother he wanted to be a football player, too.

Wilma was doubtful. Donovan was very thin, and she was afraid he would get hurt. The school coach, however, talked with Wilma and convinced her that Donovan would not get hurt. She allowed him to play.

Donovan's parents not only supported his choice to play, but they also found ways to motivate him to improve. In an article in the *Chicago Tribune*, his father remembered:

"We told him we'd give him $10 for each touchdown, and if he didn't score, he'd have extra duties in the house. That started getting a little expensive, so we broke out the $5 bills."

A Standout in High School

Donovan attended Mount Carmel High School, a Catholic school on Chicago's South Side. During his freshman year, Donovan played quarterback for the football team. In one of the games, he ran 70 yards for a touchdown. That play was called back due to a penalty, but on the next play, Donovan ran 80 yards for a touchdown, dodging defenders along the way. At that point, the coaches knew that Donovan was someone special.

In his junior year, Donovan led his team to a 12-1 record. The following year, he led them to a victory in the Chicago Prep Bowl. During his high school career, Donovan threw 27 touchdown passes to set a school record. He also set the record for most rushing yards by a quarterback, and he was named a high school All-American.

A Star in College

Many colleges were interested in enrolling Donovan, but most of them asked him to change the position he played. Donovan, however, wanted to play quarterback, and he wanted to play basketball as well. Only three schools agreed to his terms: Syracuse University in New York, the University of Iowa, and the University of Nebraska. Donovan chose Syracuse.

Washington Redskins quarterback Doug Williams drops back to pass. Williams, the first African American to quarterback a team in the Super Bowl, was a childhood hero of Donovan McNabb's.

At Syracuse, Donovan soon became known as the football team's comic. He often cracked jokes and **imitated** the coaches. One player said Donovan made him laugh so hard that he got a headache.

Donovan's humor off the field helped keep the team loose, but his teammates soon realized Donovan's play on the field was very serious. In his freshman year, he threw for 19 touchdowns and 1,776 yards.

After his sophomore year, Donovan decided to commit himself completely to football. He gave up basketball and started to hit the weight room more. He grew stronger, adding 30 pounds to his bench press. Donovan worked hard on his passing skills as well.

As a four-year starter for the Syracuse University football team, Donovan McNabb broke many school and conference records. He was named the Big East Conference's Offensive Player of the Year three consecutive seasons.

Some people viewed Donovan as mostly a running quarterback, but Donovan wanted to prove them wrong. Recalling how he felt, Donovan stated in a *Sports Illustrated* article:

> **"It really started to bother me after my redshirt freshman year. I'd pick up a preseason magazine, and they'd call me an all-purpose quarterback or an option quarterback. I can't stand that label. . . . I tried to learn more about every aspect of the passing game and take my performance to another level."**

Donovan's hard work paid off. He set Syracuse and Big East records for touchdown passes, passing yards, and total offensive yards. In his senior year, he led his team to the Orange Bowl, but Syracuse lost this game.

Unpopular Draft Pick

Most experts thought Donovan would be an early pick in the 1999 NFL draft. The Philadelphia Eagles were interested in him, but the team's fans thought their team would choose running back Ricky Williams with the first pick. Williams had set a college record for rushing yards. Even the mayor of Philadelphia, Ed Rendell, made a plea for the Eagles to draft Williams.

The word got out, however, that the Eagles were going to draft Donovan. Many fans were shocked and angry. Some traveled to the draft and booed Donovan even before the Eagles picked him. When his name was announced as the pick, they booed even more.

Donovan had heard Eagles fans could be hard on their players, but he hadn't expected this kind of response. In a *Chicago Tribune* article, Donovan said:

CROSS-CURRENTS

Read "The NFL Draft" to learn more about how pro football teams select the best college players each year. Go to page 49. ▶▶

> **"When I was booed, it definitely hurt. I look at it in a way as a motivating factor. I'm not worried about the boos."**

Donovan began his work to prove those fans wrong.

PROVING HIMSELF IN THE NFL

In 1999, Donovan signed a **contract** with the Philadelphia Eagles. The contract was worth around $54 million, and it included an $11.3 million signing bonus. Donovan was now a wealthy man, but all this money did not affect his motivation. Donovan still remembered the draft. He was determined to work hard and become the best player he could be.

In a 1999 *Chicago Tribune* article, a confident Donovan remarked:

"Despite what happened at the draft, . . . if I can go out there and strap my pads on and learn the playbook and hopefully prove to them in time, I can

Donovan McNabb was all smiles as he posed with NFL commissioner Paul Tagliabue at the 1999 NFL draft. But Donovan later admitted being hurt when Eagles fans present at the draft booed his selection by the team with the second overall pick.

change that [perception]. I think I'll be ready. If you have confidence in yourself and prepare, you can make something happen when you get in [the game].**"**

Learning to Play in the NFL

Donovan's ultimate goal, of course, was to lead the Eagles to the Super Bowl, but he also had a second goal. He knew many people thought African-American quarterbacks were good at scrambling but weren't good at passing. Donovan wanted to break that stereotype. Despite setting passing records at Syracuse, he knew he still had a lot to prove in the NFL.

The quarterback position is one of the toughest positions for young NFL players. First, they have to study and memorize a massive playbook, so they know it like the back of their hand. Then they have to adjust to the fact that the NFL game is played at a faster speed than college football.

Many talented quarterbacks don't play at all during their first season. Eagles head coach Andy Reid, however, had Donovan start six of the team's last seven games in his rookie year.

Donovan soon showed his strong throwing arm, but he had some trouble with **consistency**. He would throw a great pass and then a bad pass. Even so, Donovan led the Eagles to a victory in his first game as a starter.

Straightening Out

In the 2000 season, Donovan continued to work hard to improve his game. Progress was slow but steady. By the middle of October, Reid commented that Donovan was making the correct throw about 75 percent of the time.

Still, Donovan had a tendency to make bad throws at crucial times in games. Reid was quoted in *Sports Illustrated* as saying:

"We'll analyze [what he's doing wrong] and get it straightened out. He's very aggressive. I'll take that because in the long run it will make us better.**"**

Reid's faith in Donovan soon paid off. In a November game against the Washington Redskins, Donovan accounted for 90 percent of the Eagles' total offense. Late in the game, he led a drive that ended with a game-winning field goal. Donovan later was named NFC Player of the Week.

By the end of the 2000 season, Donovan had passed for more than 3,000 yards. He also led the team to an 11-5 record. The Eagles won six of their last seven games, including two wins in overtime.

Eagles teammates admired how calm Donovan was during tense situations in games. He would often come into the huddle and crack a joke to keep players loose. Donovan also played the comic in the locker room. This joking around included imitations of coaches,

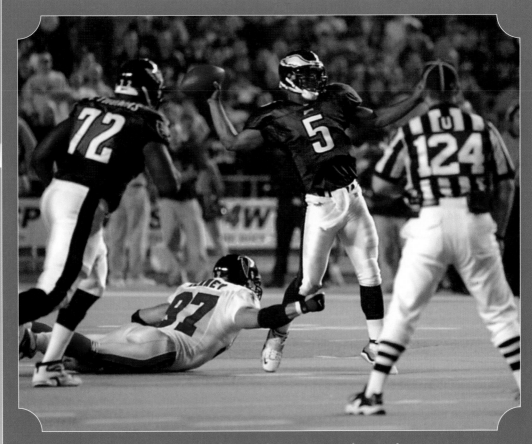

Atlanta Falcons defensive end Patrick Kerney makes a desperate attempt to stop a Donovan McNabb pass, October 1, 2000. Paced by Donovan's 311 passing yards and two touchdown throws, Philadelphia easily won the game, 38-10.

especially Reid. While imitating the head coach, Donovan would pull his pants up to his chest and then march angrily around.

Donovan also became known for his generous heart. After the terrorist attacks on the World Trade Center on September 11, 2001, he made large donations to the relief effort. In addition, Donovan started Camp for Kids Clinic. This event hosted 350 kids between the ages of 10 and 14.

Becoming a Star

By the 2001 season, Donovan had won over many of the fans who had booed him at the draft. Some even came up to him and apologized. Because Donovan loved children, he had a hard time saying no to autograph seekers. His older brother, Sean, became his bodyguard. Sean set time limits for autographs and made sure his brother wasn't **harassed**.

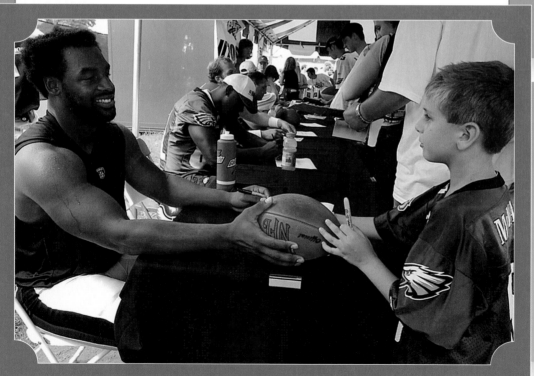

Donovan autographs a football for an eight-year-old fan at the Eagles' training camp at Lehigh University in Bethlehem, Pennsylvania, August 5, 2003. Donovan has always enjoyed taking time out to meet with kids.

Donovan performed well in 2001. He threw 25 touchdown passes and only 12 **interceptions**. He also ran for 482 yards and two touchdowns. The Eagles finished with an 11-5 record and made it into the playoffs.

In the first playoff game, against the Tampa Bay Buccaneers, Donovan threw two touchdowns, and the Eagles easily won the game, 31-9. The next week Donovan threw two more touchdown passes and ran for another score to help beat the Chicago Bears, 33-19. Next up was the NFC Championship game against the high-scoring St. Louis Rams.

The Rams were heavily favored, but the game turned out to be a close one. Donovan played well, but threw a late interception. St. Louis defeated the Eagles, 29-24.

A Tough Player

Donovan and the Eagles continued to play well the following year. In 2002, the Eagles won six of their first nine games. The game on November 17, however, started out with some concern. On the game's third play, Donovan apparently sprained his ankle, but he continued to play. Donovan ended up throwing four touchdowns in a 38-14 victory over the Arizona Cardinals.

Then surprising news came from the team. After the game, Donovan had X-rays taken of his ankle. The X-rays showed he had broken a bone. Donovan had played most of the game on a broken ankle!

Needless to say, the Eagles were crushed. The injury would probably sideline Donovan for six to eight games. The team, however, rallied around backup quarterback A.J. Feeley and made it into the playoffs.

Donovan healed quickly to return for the first playoff game. Any questions about Donovan's ankle were answered early in the game, when he avoided a rushing defensive player and ran for 19 yards. Eagles fans breathed a collective sigh of relief. Later, Donovan commented in a *Sports Illustrated* article:

> **It was no big deal, because I knew I was back. It kind of shocked me that they'd give me the opportunity to make a play like that. But I figured, if that's the way they feel, I'll roll with it.**

Donovan ended up passing for 247 yards as the Eagles defeated Atlanta, 20-6. The Eagles again made it to the NFC Championship game. This time they faced the Tampa Bay Buccaneers and their crushing defense.

Donovan and the Eagles started off well, scoring a touchdown early, but Tampa Bay answered with a touchdown of its own. Then the Eagles fumbled twice. Later, Donovan threw a costly interception. Tampa Bay won, 27-10.

The 2002 season had many highs and lows for the Eagles and their fans, but it also had some funny moments. One of these happened when Donovan's mother, Wilma, appeared in a Chunky Soup commercial with her famous son. This ad started a series of Chunky Soup commercials with Mama McNabb and Donovan.

The following year, Donovan married his college girlfriend, Roxie Nurse. He had met Roxie during his freshman year at Syracuse. Roxie had played on the women's basketball team. Donovan and Roxie later had a daughter, Alexis.

CROSS-CURRENTS

Read "Mama McNabb Makes Soup" to learn more about the popular commercials Donovan has done with his mom. Go to page 50. ▶▶

Controversial Comments

The 2003 season began with some controversy. The TV sports network ESPN had hired conservative talk-show host Rush Limbaugh as a commentator on its Sunday football pregame show. On the September 28 show, Limbaugh said that Donovan McNabb was overrated and that members of the media refrained from criticizing him because they wanted to see a black quarterback succeed. Many people thought Limbaugh's comments were racist. Donovan said he was taken aback by the comments:

CROSS-CURRENTS

To learn more about the broadcaster whose comments about Donovan McNabb in 2003 were very controversial, read "Rush Limbaugh." Go to page 51. ▶▶

❝I'm sure [Limbaugh's] not the only one that feels that way, but it's somewhat shocking to actually hear that on national TV.❞

Donovan's parents, Wilma and Sam McNabb, hold a package of Campbell's Chunky Soup before the Eagles' first regular-season game in 2001. The Eagles and Campbell Soup Company donated 5,000 cans of soup to the Philadelphia Food Bank, and Wilma McNabb would soon be starring in Campbell's commercials.

Amid the uproar, Limbaugh soon resigned from his position at ESPN. This distraction, however, did not have an effect on Donovan's performance. During the regular season, the Eagles compiled a 12-4 record. They won five games in November—the first time in Eagles history that the team had five wins in one month. Not surprisingly, Donovan was named NFL Player of the Month for November.

A Great Comeback

As the regular season ended, many people assumed the Eagles would easily make it back to the NFC Championship game. The road to this game, however, was not so easy. In the divisional

Philadelphia Eagles quarterback Donovan McNabb escapes from Green Bay Packers linebacker Hannibal Navies during third-quarter action in the NFC divisional playoffs, January 11, 2004. After converting on fourth down and 26 yards to go and tying the game late in the fourth quarter, the Eagles won in overtime, 20-17.

playoffs, the Eagles faced the Green Bay Packers, led by quarterback Brett Favre.

Favre threw two touchdown passes in the game's first quarter. The Packers led at halftime, 14-7. Late in the fourth quarter, the Packers were clinging to a 17-14 lead. With only 1 minute and 12 seconds left in the game, Donovan and his offense were at their own 26-yard line, facing fourth down and 26 yards to go. If the Eagles failed to gain 26 yards on this one play, they would lose the game—and their season would be over. In the huddle, Donovan told his players to give it all they had.

Donovan took the snap and stepped back to throw the ball. He saw wide receiver Freddie Mitchell dash across the middle of the field. Donovan threw a tight spiral. Mitchell caught the ball for a 28-yard gain and a first down. Afterward, Donovan mentioned that he knew the Packers were dropping back into pass coverage, but he just wanted to throw the ball up and allow Mitchell to make a play.

Donovan then led the Eagles into field-goal range. With five seconds left, David Akers tied the score with a 37-yard field goal. In overtime, Favre threw an interception that set up a game-winning field goal for the Eagles.

This game was one of the greatest comebacks in the history of the Philadelphia Eagles. **Momentum** seemed to be on the Eagles' side as they headed into another NFC Championship game, this time against the Carolina Panthers.

The Panthers, however, had a strong defense. They forced Donovan to throw three interceptions. Later, Donovan injured his rib cage and left the game. The Panthers ran the ball well and ended up winning, 14-3.

Some people wondered if Donovan and the Eagles would ever get over the hump and win the NFC Championship. Three times this game had proven to be a roadblock to the Super Bowl. Would this roadblock ever be overcome? The next season would provide the answer.

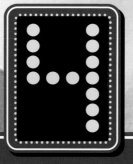

CONTROVERSY AND INJURIES

Donovan and the Eagles had a great season in 2004. The addition of Terrell Owens seemed to be exactly what the Eagles needed. Donovan and Terrell hit it off, both on and off the field. Donovan threw for 3,875 yards and 31 touchdowns, and T.O. caught 77 passes and had 14 touchdowns.

Finally, the Eagles got over their playoff hump and won the NFC Championship. Their loss to the Patriots in the Super Bowl was a disappointment, but the team still faced the next season with high hopes.

Problems with Terrell Owens

Soon after the Super Bowl, however, T.O. began to complain about his contract. T.O. had a seven-year contract worth about

$49 million. He had played only one year, so six years were left on the contract. Even so, T.O. felt he was underpaid, and he wanted to **renegotiate** his deal.

Before long, a media storm swirled around this story. In the middle of this controversy, Owens and some teammates added fuel to the fire. They claimed that Donovan had been tired during the Super Bowl. In an interview on April 29, 2005, Donovan responded to these remarks:

Donovan McNabb drops back to pass during the Pro Bowl, Honolulu, Hawaii, February 13, 2005. The 2004 season had been Donovan's best by far, and his excellent play won him the honor of being the NFC's starting quarterback in the Pro Bowl.

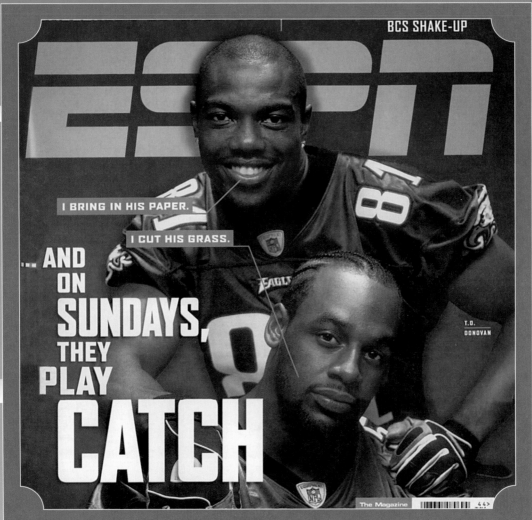

BCS SHAKE-UP

ESPN

I BRING IN HIS PAPER.

I CUT HIS GRASS.

...AND ON SUNDAYS, THEY PLAY CATCH

T.O.
DONOVAN

The Magazine

When the October 25, 2004, issue of *ESPN the Magazine* hit newsstands, Donovan McNabb and Terrell Owens had played together for six games—and already connected on eight touchdown passes. The apparently warm relationship between the two would be severely strained by season's end, however.

> **"I wasn't tired. . . . I don't even know what play or what series they were talking about me being tired, but all I know is that we scored to pretty much put ourselves up in the game. And if they were talking about towards the end of the game, I really don't know what they're talking about."**

Donovan went on to say that if anyone had a problem with him, they should deal with him directly. Despite this response, the controversy would not go away.

Owens continued to complain about his contract, and he was suspended for a week during training camp. To make matters worse, star running back Brian Westbrook had a seven-day **holdout**, and the Eagles released Corey Simon, a talented defensive player.

Soon experts and fans had questions about the Eagles. Would all of this controversy distract from the team's chemistry? Would the problems between Donovan and T.O. affect their performance on the field? In a *Sports Illustrated* article, Donovan assured fans that the problems would have no effect:

> **On the field I'm going to do everything I can to make things work. Whatever communication [Owens and I] have to have to make the offense work, we'll have. Our relationship on the field is one of the best in the NFL.**

Head coach Andy Reid was confident that Donovan could keep the team stable. Some wondered why Reid didn't just cut T.O., but Reid knew that the talented wide receiver added a lot to the team. T.O. was one of the most explosive receivers in the league. Without him, the Eagles' offense would be much less dangerous.

An Up-and-Down Season

In 2005, the Eagles lost their opening game to the Atlanta Falcons, 14-10. In the following game, however, the Eagles seemed to be back to their old selves. They crushed the San Francisco 49ers, 42-3. Donovan threw five touchdown passes, and two of them were to Owens. In total, the offense gained 583 yards, a team record. Meanwhile, the team's defense allowed only 142 total yards. They also recorded three interceptions and three **sacks**.

At the end of the game against San Francisco, Donovan and T.O. were joking and laughing together. Their relationship seemed fine, and the team appeared headed in the right direction. Wins over the Oakland Raiders and Kansas City Chiefs seemed to confirm this impression.

The Eagles, however, lost two of their next three games. In the two losses, they were completely outplayed. Then, in the first week of November, T.O. made more controversial comments. During an interview, he said the Eagles would be better if Green Bay's Brett Favre was their quarterback instead of Donovan. He also said he was upset that the Eagles didn't celebrate his 100th career touchdown.

CROSS-CURRENTS

Read "Terrell Owens" to learn more about the talented but controversial wide receiver who played for Philadelphia in 2004 and 2005. Go to page 52. ▶▶

Later, Owens apologized for his remarks. Some Eagles teammates said Donovan and T.O. would resolve their problems. Team officials, however, had had enough. On November 5, they suspended Owens. A few days later, Reid stated:

"Terrell Owens has been suspended by the team for four games for conduct detrimental to the team. He will not be returning to play for the team even after the conclusion of that suspension."

This controversy caused a media frenzy. Meanwhile, Donovan and the Eagles tried their best to turn the season around.

The Eagles lost a hard-fought game to the Washington Redskins, 17-10. The next week, against Dallas, Donovan suffered a groin injury and had to leave the game. The Eagles lost, 21-20.

Donovan had played much of the year with a painful condition called a sports hernia, which now required surgery. He would miss the rest of the season. Without Donovan, the Eagles went on to lose five of their last seven games. Their final record was 6-10. As a result, they missed the playoffs for the first time in six years.

The season had begun with so much promise. Donovan and Terrell Owens had been almost unstoppable in 2004. A year later, their relationship was poisoned. T.O. had missed nine games because of his suspension, and Donovan had lost seven games to injury. Fans wondered whether the team could recover in 2006.

Improving Team Chemistry

During the off-season, the Eagles released Owens, and he signed a contract with the Dallas Cowboys. Even though the troublesome

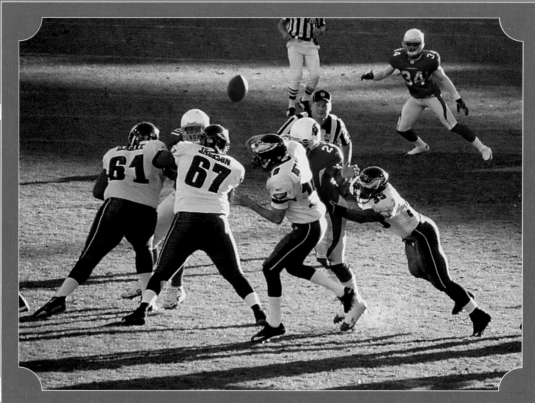

With Donovan McNabb lost to injury in mid-November 2005, the Eagles went into a tailspin, managing just two wins in the final seven games of the season. Here, backup quarterback Koy Detmer is hit as he releases the ball during Philadelphia's December 24 loss to the Arizona Cardinals.

T.O. was now gone, some Eagles players still had hard feelings about the season. Donovan tried to heal these wounds in various ways.

Though he couldn't play or practice after his sports-hernia surgery, Donovan continued to show up at the Eagles' complex during his rehab. Doing this allowed him to spend more time with his teammates. Many players appreciated Donovan's efforts to improve the team's chemistry. In a *Sports Illustrated* article, tight end L.J. Smith commented:

> **Donovan doesn't have to tell you he's a leader—his actions speak louder than his words—but for him to be around the guys, I think that's his best therapy.**

Before training camp in 2006, Donovan held his annual boot camp at his home. During this time, players went through a hard workout under the guidance of a trainer. At the end, Donovan threw a huge cookout, New Orleans style. Players were welcome to invite their wives, girlfriends, and children to this event.

When training camp started, Donovan continued to keep players loose with his jokes. In fact, he often imitated Reid before team meetings.

Then, five days before the start of the season, Donovan held a skill-players practice. Skill players include wide receivers, running backs, and tight ends. Coaches were not invited to this practice. Without coaches, players were allowed to freely voice their concerns about the offense.

At first, Donovan's efforts to bring the players together produced results. In the opening game of the 2006 season, Donovan threw for 314 yards and three touchdowns. The Eagles soundly defeated the Houston Texans, 24-10, and Donovan was named Player of the Week.

The Eagles' hot streak continued, and they won three of their next four games. During this four-game span, Donovan threw for more than 1,200 yards and eight touchdowns without suffering a single interception.

Dealing with Criticism and Injury

Donovan and the Eagles then hit a rough patch. They lost two games by a field goal and a third game by a touchdown. Donovan received a lot of criticism for the Eagles' performance. A member of the prominent civil-rights group the NAACP (National Association for the Advancement of Colored People) wrote an article that called Donovan a mediocre quarterback. Then a newspaper columnist suggested that the Eagles bench Donovan.

Some fans were surprised by the harsh response. Donovan's performance in the three losses had not been good, but he remained one of the leading passers in the NFL. In his first seven seasons, he had thrown 134 touchdowns and only 66 interceptions. Donovan also had the best winning percentage among active NFL quarterbacks.

Even so, Donovan continually received criticism in Philadelphia. In 2006, there appeared to be even more criticism. In a November 20,

Donovan McNabb passes a glass of milk to Patriots linebacker Tedy Bruschi. The two football stars, opponents in Super Bowl XXXIX, teamed up for the "Got Milk?" ad campaign.

2006, *Sports Illustrated* article, former Eagles quarterback Ron Jaworski discussed the pressure that Donovan got from Eagles fans:

❝Donovan has always done everything the right way. He's the Tiger Woods of the NFL: He has a great family; he has never screwed up off the field. Those guys always deserve the benefit of the doubt. But for whatever reason, Donovan doesn't get it.❞

Donovan responded by simply trying to ignore the criticism. Some people liked that, and some did not. Donovan, however, was not about to change how he approached the game.

Wearing the jersey of their favorite player, youth from the Boys & Girls Clubs of Philadelphia pose for a photo, June 10, 2006. They had just participated in Donovan McNabb's All-Star Kids Clinic.

After the three losses, Donovan and the Eagles got back on track in the next game. They soundly defeated the Washington Redskins, 27-3. The following game, against the Tennessee Titans, Donovan was dealt a crushing blow. He tore his anterior cruciate **ligament** (ACL) and was out for the season. In the first nine games of the season, Donovan had been second in the NFL in passing yards and passing touchdowns. Without him, the Eagles scored only 13 points and lost to the Titans.

CROSS-CURRENTS

To learn more about ACL tears and other ailments common among NFL players, read "Football Injuries." Go to page 53. ▶▶

To the Eagles' credit, they rallied around backup quarterback Jeff Garcia. The team won its last five games and made it to the playoffs. After beating the New York Giants in the first round, the Eagles lost to the New Orleans Saints.

Offering Help off the Field

Donovan remained a popular figure off the field. He was paid to endorse products ranging from health drinks to athletic shoes to credit cards. The companies that hired Donovan as a spokesperson for their products also agreed to support the Donovan McNabb Foundation.

This foundation continues to give money to the American Diabetes Association. In addition, it sponsors a camp for children with diabetes. The foundation also hosts a football school, in which children receive free instruction on how to play the game from Donovan and other NFL players.

Donovan has supported many other groups, including the American Red Cross and a children's medical center. He has also given time and money in support of his high school and college.

All of these positive activities, however, didn't make up for Donovan's tough season in 2006. It is very difficult to recover from an ACL tear. Some players never come back from this type of injury. Donovan knew he had his work cut out for him in the off-season.

RUMORS AND RECOVERY

During the 2007 off-season, Donovan's knee injury seemed to be healing properly. However, questions about his ability to come back and play still surfaced. Some quarterbacks get nervous when they return to the game after tearing an ACL. Would Donovan's injury heal completely? Would he be able to maintain his high level of play?

A Controversial Draft Pick

These questions became more intense when draft day arrived. With their first selection of the 2007 draft, the Eagles picked a quarterback, Kevin Kolb. Kolb had an outstanding career in

Wearing a brace on his right knee, Donovan McNabb drops back to pass during Eagles training camp, July 31, 2007. As the 2007 season approached, fans and football insiders alike wondered how effective Donovan would be after his ACL injury.

college. He went to the University of Houston, where he started at quarterback for four years. In his senior year, Kolb threw 30 touchdowns and had just four interceptions.

Experts and fans were stunned by the pick. Did this mean that the Eagles had lost faith in Donovan? Was his injury worse than people knew? Even Donovan himself admitted that he had been surprised by the Eagles draft.

Apparently, Donovan first heard the news in an ice cream shop. In an interview for the Eagles Web site on May 8, 2007, Donovan described how he felt.

CROSS-CURRENTS

To learn more about Donovan McNabb's new backup quarterback with the Philadelphia Eagles, read "Kevin Kolb." Go to page 53. ▶▶

"It was shocking first and foremost, but again my job is to focus in on my rehab and lead this team to a Super Bowl. . . . [My wife] said that we took a quarterback. My reaction was 'Wow on our first pick? Yeah, well okay that's something.' And then you just keep getting ice cream and ordering sprinkles for your daughter."

Trade Rumors

Donovan went on to say that Coach Reid had assured him that he was still the team's starting quarterback. Rumors, however, continued to spread that Donovan's days as an Eagle were numbered.

These rumors received a boost in June 2007. Tommie Harris, a defensive tackle for the Chicago Bears, said he wanted Donovan to be the quarterback for the Bears instead of the often-criticized Rex

Kevin Kolb in action for the University of Houston. When the Eagles selected the quarterback with their first pick in the 2007 NFL draft, many fans began to wonder whether Donovan McNabb's days in Philadelphia were numbered.

Grossman. Harris also said he thought the Bears could win the Super Bowl with Donovan leading them.

Harris was a good friend of Donovan's. Soon rumors surfaced that the Eagles were planning to trade Donovan to the Bears. Then, in an article on the Bears' Web site, Harris claimed that he was only joking:

> **"Donovan and I were joking the whole day. Donovan was behind the cameras laughing. We were joking around. It escalated to more than it was. I apologized to my team. I was very embarrassed how much it blew up. My team forgave me; that's all that matters."**

The media, however, continued to take the trade rumors seriously. During training camp, Donovan and his teammates tried to focus as much as possible on football.

Then, Donovan made some surprising remarks. On a television show, Donovan said that black quarterbacks get more criticism than white quarterbacks. The only exception to this, he said, might be the Bears' quarterback, Rex Grossman. Later Donovan explained that he thought black quarterbacks had to do a little more to prove themselves. In a *Chicago Tribune* article on September 20, 2007, he stated:

> **"I never said Peyton [Manning] doesn't get criticized. I never said Carson [Palmer] doesn't get criticized. I never said Tom [Brady] doesn't get criticized, because they do. We get criticized a little differently."**

All in all, during the 2007 off-season, there were injury questions, trade rumors, and controversial comments. Good news, however, came concerning Donovan's injury. His recovery was ahead of schedule.

The Long Road Back

The first two games of the 2007 season didn't go well. The Eagles lost a close game to Green Bay, 16-13. They followed that with another close loss, this time to Washington.

Donovan struggled during both games. He used to be able to easily avoid defenders, but now his **mobility** was limited. His throws, too, weren't very accurate. The knee injury was hindering his play.

The next game celebrated the 75th anniversary of the Eagles franchise. The Eagles played the Detroit Lions. Donovan and his offense celebrated the occasion in grand style. In the first 30 minutes, the offense gained 473 yards and scored 42 points. This set a team record.

Donovan completed 21 of 26 passes. He also threw four touchdowns. It was one of the best games of his career. The Eagles ended up crushing the Lions, 56-21.

Donovan and the Eagles seemed to be back in business, but in the next two games, they played inconsistently. They lost to the New York Giants and then beat the New York Jets.

The following game was against the Bears. The first half of this game was close, but then Donovan led a fourth quarter drive for a touchdown. The Eagles were ahead, 16-12, with only 1 minute and 52 seconds left in the game. The Bears got the ball on their own 3-yard line, so they had to go 97 yards to score. A win for the Eagles seemed to be in the bag.

Then the unthinkable happened. Led by quarterback Brian Griese, the Bears marched down the field. With 15 seconds left, Chicago reached the Eagles' 15-yard line. Griese threw a touchdown pass, and the Bears won, 19-16.

It was a tough loss for Donovan and the Eagles, but Donovan rallied his teammates. The Eagles won two of their next three games. Maybe the Eagles' season could still be saved.

Another Injury

The next game, however, started off rough for Donovan, and then it got worse. The Miami Dolphins intercepted two of his passes. Donovan completed only three of his first 11 passes. Then, on a blitz play, a Dolphins cornerback chased Donovan.

Donovan threw the ball out of bounds and was then tackled. When he got up, he limped to the sidelines. After talking to the trainers, Donovan went to the locker room. He had a sprained ankle and would miss at least two games. Led by their defense, the Eagles managed to defeat the Dolphins, 17-7, but without Donovan the team lost the next two games.

One of these losses was against the undefeated New England Patriots. Many experts were calling the Patriots the best team ever.

Donovan McNabb scans the Buffalo Bills' defense, December 30, 2007. The Eagles won, 17-9, capping a three-game winning streak at the end of the 2007 season. Steadier play by Donovan McNabb gave Eagles fans hope that the quarterback would return to pre-injury form in 2008.

more relaxed. In an article on the Eagles Web site on April 10, 2008, Donovan commented:

> **It's always good when you can focus in on each element of your game and take the necessary steps to move forward to become a better football player, instead of recovering from an injury. I have a free mind. I'm focusing on my speed, my footwork and my strength and my flexibility instead of going through rehab and trying to strengthen the part of your body that isn't right.**

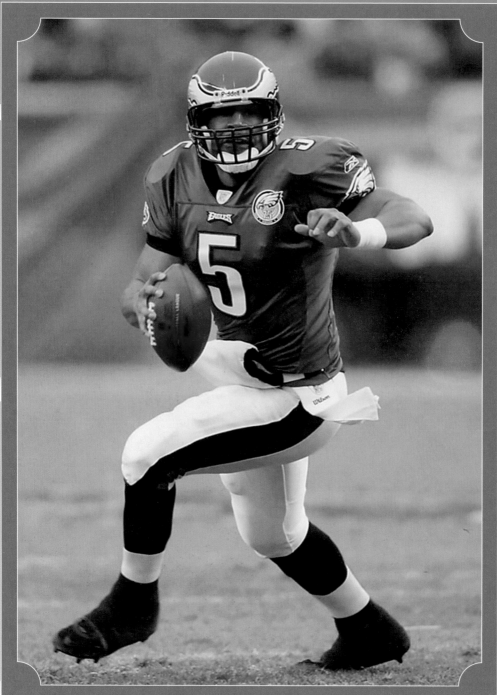

As the 2008 season approached, Philadelphia Eagles fans were hoping that a healthy and rejuvenated Donovan McNabb could lead the team back to the Super Bowl.

The Past and the Future

Looking back on his career, Donovan has a lot to be proud of. At the start of the 2008 season, he was second among Eagles quarterbacks for career touchdown passes, with 171. (Ron Jaworski held the Eagles' record for touchdown passes, with 175.) Donovan was also poised to replace Jaworski as the Eagles' all-time leader in passing yards. Jaworski amassed 26,963 passing yards; Donovan entered the 2008 season with 25,404 yards.

In addition, Donovan had led the Eagles to five NFC East titles as of 2008. In the playoffs, he went to the NFC Championship game four times, and he made it to the Super Bowl once.

Instead of looking back, however, Donovan is looking forward. He is convinced that the 2008 season will be a great one for the Eagles. Donovan stated in an article on the Eagles Web site:

"We're working hard. . . . I'm excited. I'm focused on this team and this season, and I can't wait to get it started. We're going to take what we did at the end of last season and build on it and get rolling right from the start this year."

Donovan's positive attitude continues with his charities. He again took part in the "NFL Take a Player to School" event. Donovan has been a part of this program since 2003.

Both on and off the field, Donovan has proven to be a positive influence.

CROSS-CURRENTS

Read "NFL Take a Player to School" to learn more about a charitable program that Donovan has been involved with. Go to page 54. ▶▶

Falcons Quarterback Michael Vick

Michael Vick was born on June 26, 1980, in Newport News, Virginia. He grew up in this city and attended college at Virginia Tech. He soon became the starting quarterback on the Hokies, Virginia Tech's football team. In 1999, he led the Hokies to college football's national championship game. The Hokies, however, lost this game.

Vick was the top overall pick of the 2001 NFL draft. His team, the Atlanta Falcons, thought they had signed a player with great potential. At first, their hopes seemed justified. In 2002, Vick set the record for the most rushing yards in a game by a quarterback. Vick went on to lead the Falcons to the playoffs in 2002 and 2004.

Then, in 2007, shocking news hit the NFL and the nation. On July 17, Vick and three other people were charged with organizing dogfights. The charges included killing dogs that didn't perform well in the fights. Gambling was also connected to the dogfighting.

On August 24, Vick pleaded guilty, and the NFL soon suspended him. The length of the suspension was not given. On December 10, Vick was sentenced to 23 months in federal prison. Soon afterward, several states strengthened their animal cruelty laws. (Go back to page 6.) ◀◀

Quarterback Michael Vick appeared headed for stardom when the Atlanta Falcons drafted him with the first overall pick in 2001. By 2007, however, Vick was out of football and serving time in a federal prison.

The Super Bowl

The National Football League (NFL) championship game is called the Super Bowl. In this game, the American Football Conference (AFC) champion plays the National Football Conference (NFC) champion.

The game was conceived in 1966 when a merger was planned between the NFL and the American Football League (AFL). The game was first called the AFL-NFL World Championship Game, and it quickly attracted national attention.

The term "Super Bowl" was first used in 1969, and Roman numerals were attached to each Super Bowl. The Super Bowl played in February 2008, for example, was called Super Bowl XLII (42).

The Super Bowl has developed into an unofficial national holiday. People often throw Super Bowl parties and gather friends and family to watch the game. Many taverns and restaurants also have Super Bowl celebrations.

During the week before the game, the media focuses much of its attention on the two teams. The Super Bowl itself gets high television ratings. As a result, many companies pay much more money than usual for commercial time during the game. In 2005, a 30-second commercial during the game cost $2.4 million.

Commercials shown during the game are usually new and very creative. They often receive a lot of attention from the media and public. In fact, this attention almost rivals the attention given to the game itself. (Go back to page 8.) ◀◀

In the United States—and, increasingly, around the world—Super Bowl Sunday is a time for parties. This 2007 photo captured party preparations at a restaurant in Miami before Super Bowl XLI, which pitted the Chicago Bears against the Indianapolis Colts.

Donovan's Fight Against Diabetes

During Donovan's childhood, his grandmother died from diabetes. Donovan's father also has diabetes. Later, Donovan became a strong supporter of the American Diabetes Association (ADA), an association that works to prevent and treat diabetes and research a cure for this disease.

Diabetes is a disease that has two general forms: diabetes insipidus and diabetes mellitus. Diabetes mellitus, the more common form, is divided further into two types.

Type I often starts in childhood. With this type, the body is unable to produce insulin, a **hormone** that controls the level of glucose (sugar) found in the blood. Type II usually strikes people who are over 40. People with this type have a body that either produces insulin at a slow rate or doesn't respond well to insulin. With both types, insulin problems cause the body's glucose level to rise, so people have too much sugar in their bloodstream.

People often discover they have diabetes when they become unusually thirsty and urinate a lot. Diabetes can kill a person if it goes untreated. With the proper treatment, however, diabetes can be controlled. To control the disease, people with diabetes are put on diets that limit the amount of sugar and fat they can eat. They can also take insulin to control glucose levels. They are also told to exercise regularly. Exercise helps glucose move into the body's muscles. (Go back to page 11.) ◄◄

Diabetic student Morgan Thompson, of West Bloomfield, Michigan, shows former NBA player Chris Dudley his blood glucose results, November 14, 2006. Dudley, who is also diabetic, visited Morgan's middle school on World Diabetes Day to raise awareness of the disease.

The NFL Draft

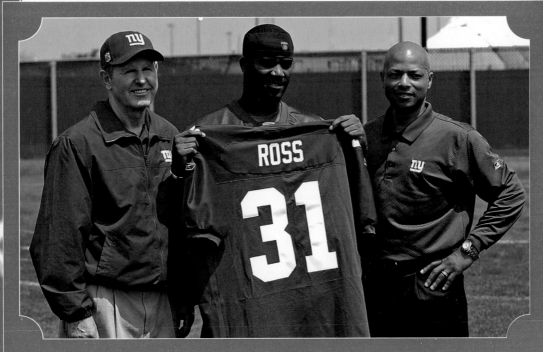

New York Giants head coach Tom Coughlin (left) and general manager Jerry Reese (right) pose for a photo with the team's 2007 first-round draft pick, cornerback Aaron Ross, May 12, 2007.

The NFL brings new players into the league through a process known as the draft. The draft is organized into a series of seven rounds. In each round, each of the 32 NFL teams gets to pick a player.

The order in which teams pick is determined by their success the previous year. The team with the worst record gets the first choice. The team with the second-worst record gets the second choice, and so on. The Super Bowl winner gets the last pick of the round. The draft is organized this way to try to balance the talent levels among the teams.

Teams can change the order of their pick, however, if they trade a player. The Super Bowl winner, for example, could trade a star player for a higher pick.

A team can greatly improve its performance if it makes a series of good picks. On the other hand, several bad picks can affect the team's performance for years. To make sure they make a good pick, teams spend lots of time researching players, and players are asked to perform a series of drills and tests.

The draft takes place near the end of April, and it is a huge media event. The top players usually attend and dress well for the event. When players are picked, fans cheer or boo the selections. (Go back to page 15.) ◄◄

Mama McNabb Makes Soup

Donovan McNabb's mother, Wilma, worked for years as a registered nurse. She also spent a lot of time in the kitchen preparing meals for her family. Back then, Wilma never thought she would be shown making soup on television.

After Donovan became a football star, however, he started to do Chunky soup commercials. At first, an actress played his mother, but then Wilma had a brainstorm. She thought she could do these commercials with her son. Eventually, Campbell's, the company that makes Chunky, agreed.

Wilma, known as Mama McNabb, did her first Chunky soup commercial in 2002. The ad was an instant success. Many fans were already familiar with her since she was often shown in the stands during Eagles games. Other ads soon followed. In one commercial, Mama McNabb serves soup to Eagles players. In another, she tells players to avoid junk food. She even gets water dumped on her from a bucket. In the first three years that these commercials were shown, sales for Chunky soup increased by 40 percent.

The commercials are part fantasy and part reality. Wilma actually does prepare meals for Eagles players when they come to Chicago. (Go back to page 22.)

Texas A&M offensive lineman Alan Reuber pulls Donovan and Wilma McNabb in a competition for charity sponsored by Campbell's Chunky Soup, January 27, 2004. Since 2002, Wilma McNabb has done commercials for Chunky.

Rush Limbaugh

Rush Limbaugh is a commentator for television and radio shows. Limbaugh also has his own radio talk show on which he voices his opinions. He has many fans, but his opinions are often very controversial.

Limbaugh was born in Cape Girardeau, Missouri, in 1951, and he has two younger brothers. He was interested in radio during his childhood. As an adult, Limbaugh worked at radio stations in Pittsburgh, Pennsylvania, and Kansas City, Missouri.

Limbaugh was fired from both of those jobs because his bosses didn't like him expressing his controversial views on the air. Eventually, Limbaugh found a job at a radio station in Sacramento, California. This station was looking for a controversial broadcaster. Limbaugh's show soon became a hit. He then began hosting a national radio talk show in New York City.

Limbaugh is known for having many loyal followers. Many people also dislike him and his views. His followers go by the nickname "ditto-heads." Limbaugh's 1993 book *See, I Told You So* had a first printing of 20 million copies. In the 1990s, Limbaugh was inducted into the Radio Hall of Fame.

Limbaugh has been married and divorced several times. After an unsuccessful back surgery, Limbaugh started taking pain medication, and he became addicted to this medication. He has since received treatment for the addiction. (Go back to page 22.)

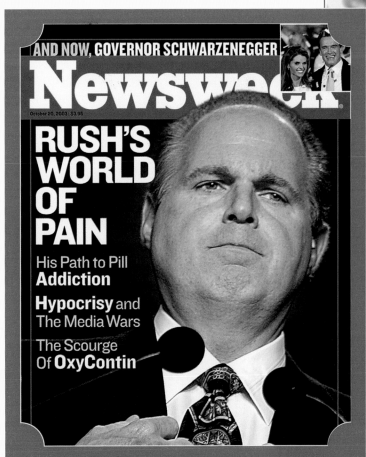

The October 20, 2003, cover of Newsweek *magazine featured Rush Limbaugh. Ten days earlier, the controversial radio talk-show host had admitted his addiction to a prescription painkiller, and authorities in Florida were investigating whether Limbaugh had obtained the medications illegally.*

Terrell Owens

Terrell Owens (T.O.) has caused controversy throughout his football career. Owens, a talented athlete, lettered in four sports in high school. After scoring his first touchdown there, he did a celebration dance for his mother.

T.O. would do many more touchdown celebrations in his career. Owens went to college in Tennessee, where he became a star player. In 1996, the San Francisco 49ers drafted him as a wide receiver. Owens was thrilled. His favorite player, Jerry Rice, played for San Francisco.

Owens soon showed his talent. In 1999, he caught an NFL-record 20 passes in one game. In 2000, however, he did a touchdown dance on the Dallas Cowboys' midfield logo. This gesture was considered a sign of disrespect. Soon after this, Owens claimed his head coach intentionally lost a game because he was a friend of the opposing coach.

Actions like these created controversy for Owens. In 2002, he added fuel to the fire. After scoring a touchdown, he signed a football with a Sharpie. In response, the NFL passed a rule that prohibits players from using foreign objects on the field. This rule became known as the "Sharpie rule."

T.O. became dissatisfied with the 49ers, so they traded him to Philadelphia. Controversy continued to follow T.O. in his new home. After two years, Philadelphia released Owens, and he signed with Dallas. (Go back to page 30.) ◀◀

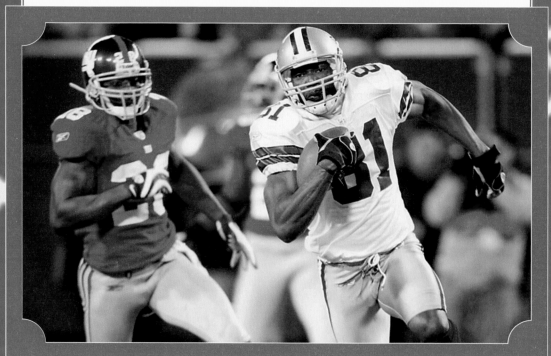

Dallas Cowboys wide receiver Terrell Owens runs away from New York Giants safety Gibril Wilson in action from 2007. Wherever he has gone, the flamboyant Owens has created controversy.

Football Injuries

Football is a rough sport, and many players can be injured during play. These injuries cover a wide range, and some of them can end a player's career.

One of the more serious injuries is the ACL tear. The ACL is a ligament that connects the thigh bone to the shin bone. This ligament helps control the knee's movement. It keeps the shin bone from moving too far forward. In football, the ACL is often torn when a player is struck in the knee while he is moving.

Injuries to the neck are also dangerous. Recently, coaches have been stressing proper tackling methods to reduce these injuries.

The "sports hernia" is another severe injury. This injury is the tearing or straining of muscles in the lower abdomen just above the groin—the area where the thigh meets the hips. Other common injuries include hamstring strains and tears, ankle sprains, and cramping.

Football players wear pads and helmets for protection, but the helmets can also cause injuries. If a player leads with his helmet when he tackles, the helmet can cause serious injury to the tackled player. Injuries can also occur when players tackling each other hit their helmets together. (Go back to page 35.) ◀◀

Kevin Kolb

Kevin Kolb was born in Stephenville, Texas, on August 24, 1984. Kevin's father ran an RV park and also coached football and basketball in middle school. His mother taught the sixth grade. Kevin has a sister who also coached basketball.

While growing up, Kevin had many jobs. Some of them included cleaning carpets, building fences, and working in a nursery. In addition, Kevin used to play for his father's football and basketball teams.

In high school, Kevin was a standout quarterback. He threw for 29 touchdowns in his senior year and received first-team All–Big County honors. He almost went to Oklahoma State, but he changed his mind and instead attended the University of Houston. One reason for this change was that his high school coach accepted a job at Houston.

Kevin continued to excel as a quarterback in college. He is now married and lives with his wife, Whitney, in Granbury, Texas. Whitney is also an athlete, and she played on her golf team in college. Kevin and his wife golf, fish, play tennis, and hunt. (Go back to page 37.) ◀◀

NFL Take a Player to School

The "NFL Take a Player to School" program makes the wish of 34 young fans come true. Every year, from July to September, more than 100,000 children between the ages of 6 and 13 enter this contest. Children enter by mailing in an entry form or entering online at the NFL's Web site or the Web site of J.C. Penney, another contest sponsor. Out of these entries, 34 fans win, one from each NFL team and two from areas that do not have a local team.

The winners each receive a visit from a player on their favorite NFL team. Many star players take part in this program, including Michael Strahan, Antonio Gates, and Donovan McNabb. Winners also receive an NFL jersey, hat, and T-shirt.

The visit starts at the winner's home, with the player meeting the family. The player is then given a tour of the home. After this, the winner and the player take a limousine ride to the winner's school. There they are greeted by teachers and classmates. Then the player shares football stories with children at the school. The player also stresses the importance of exercise. Players tell children that they should exercise at least 60 minutes a day. (Go back to page 45.) ◀◀

Carolina Panthers wide receiver Steve Smith visits Weddington Christian Academy in Weddington, North Carolina, as part of the NFL's Take a Player to School program.

1976   Donovan McNabb is born on November 25 in Chicago.

Early 1990s   Donovan attends Mount Carmel High School, where he plays quarterback and leads his team to Chicago's Prep Bowl championship.

1999   Donovan leads his college team, the Syracuse Orangemen, to the Orange Bowl, where they are defeated by the University of Florida on January 2.

On April 17, the Philadelphia Eagles select Donovan in the first round of the NFL draft with the second overall pick.

2002   Donovan and the Eagles lose the NFC Championship game to the St. Louis Rams on January 27.

2003   Donovan and the Eagles lose the NFC Championship game to the Tampa Bay Buccaneers on January 19.

Donovan marries Roxie Nurse.

2004   Donovan leads one of the greatest comebacks in the history of the Eagles, as the Eagles defeat the Green Bay Packers in the NFC Divisional Playoffs on January 11.

Donovan and the Eagles lose the NFC Championship game to the Carolina Panthers on January 18.

2005   Donovan leads the Eagles to an NFC Championship with a victory over the Atlanta Falcons on January 23.

Donovan and the Eagles are defeated by the New England Patriots in Super Bowl XXXIX on February 6.

Donovan suffers a groin injury in a game against the Dallas Cowboys on November 14.

2006   Donovan tears his ACL in a game against the Tennessee Titans on November 19.

2007   Donovan and the Eagles celebrate the team's 75th anniversary by defeating the Detroit Lions, 56-21, on September 23.

Career Statistics

Year	Team	G	Att	Comp	Pct	Yds	TD	Int	Rating
1999	Philadelphia Eagles	12	216	106	49.1	948	8	7	60.1
2000	Philadelphia Eagles	16	569	330	58.0	3,365	21	13	77.8
2001	Philadelphia Eagles	16	493	285	57.8	3,233	25	12	84.3
2002	Philadelphia Eagles	10	361	211	58.4	2,289	17	6	86.0
2003	Philadelphia Eagles	16	478	275	57.5	3,216	16	11	79.6
2004	Philadelphia Eagles	15	469	300	64.0	3,875	31	8	104.7
2005	Philadelphia Eagles	9	357	211	59.1	2,507	16	9	85.0
2006	Philadelphia Eagles	10	316	180	57.0	2,647	18	6	95.5
2007	Philadelphia Eagles	14	473	291	61.5	3,324	19	7	89.9
Total		118	3,732	2,189	58.7	25,404	171	79	85.8

Awards and Accomplishments

2000 NFL Player of the Year by CBS Radio All-Madden Team

2001 NFL Pro Bowl

2002 NFC Offensive Player of the Month
NFL Pro Bowl
Wanamaker Award

2003 NFC Offensive Player of the Month
NFL Pro Bowl
Most Caring Athlete by *USA Weekend* Magazine
NFL Man of the Year Finalist

2004 Eagles record for highest quarterback rating, completion percentage, and passing yards
NFL record 24 consecutive completions
NFC Offensive Player of the Month
NFL Pro Bowl
NFL Players Association Perseverance Award
Children's Crisis Treatment Center Honor

2005 NFC Offensive Player of the Month
NFL Pro Bowl
NFL Man of the Year Finalist

Books

Bradley, Michael. *Donovan McNabb*. New York: Benchmark Books, 2004.

Mattern, Joanne. *Donovan McNabb: Football Star*. Hockessin, DE: Mitchell Lane Publishers, 2004.

Preller, James. *National Football League Superstars*. New York: Scholastic, 2003.

Robinson, Tom. *Donovan McNabb: Leader On and Off the Field*. Berkeley Heights, NJ: Enslow Publishers, 2007.

Steenkamer, Paul. *Sports Great Donovan McNabb*. Berkeley Heights, NJ: Enslow Publishers, 2003.

Periodicals

Bradley, John. "Eagle Scout." *Sports Illustrated* vol. 95, no. 4 (July 30, 2001): p. 58–70.

Gregory, Sean. "Donovan's Revenge." *Time* vol. 165, no. 6 (February 7, 2005): p. 69.

King, Peter. "Super Effort." *Sports Illustrated* vol. 102, no. 4 (January 31, 2005): p. 42–45.

Silver, Michael. "McNificent." *Sports Illustrated* vol. 100, no. 2 (January 19, 2004): p. 48–54.

Web Sites

http://www.philadelphiaeagles.com/

The official Web site of the Philadelphia Eagles provides biographical information and statistics about Donovan McNabb and other Eagles players.

http://www.nfl.com/

The official Web site of the NFL provides statistics about Donovan McNabb and other NFL players, both past and present.

http://www.donovanmcnabb.com/

The official Web site of Donovan McNabb gives information about Donovan's business ventures, family, and charities.

http://www.diabetes.org/

The official Web site of the American Diabetes Association describes Donovan's involvement with the organization.

http://www.jointheteam.com/

The official Web site of the NFL Join the Team organization describes programs that this group sponsors and includes an article about the "Take a Player to School" program.

The Web sites mentioned in this book were active at the time of publication. The publisher is not responsible for Web sites that have changed their addresses or discontinued operation since the date of publication. The publisher will review and update the Web site addresses each time the book is reprinted.

consistency—the ability to perform a task over and over with little variation or difference in the performance.

contract—an agreement between two parties. In the NFL, these agreements are between players and teams and involve decisions on how many years the player will play for a specific team and how much the team will pay the player.

controversy—a matter of opinion over which several people or parties disagree; a dispute.

double-teaming—having two defensive players guard one offensive player.

ecstatic—having the feeling of great joy.

execute—to carry out or perform an action, especially one that requires skill.

harass—to repeatedly annoy or bother someone.

holdout—the act of resisting or waiting for something you desire without giving in. In the NFL, players can threaten a holdout and not participate in practices or games until the player's team agrees to talk with the player and agree on a new contract or listen to the player's demands.

hormone—a chemical the body produces that travels through the blood and helps control certain body functions.

imitate—to copy a person's or animal's behavior; mimic.

interception—the stealing of a pass, usually thrown by the quarterback, by a member of the opposing team's defense.

ligament—a flexible, fibrous tissue in the body that connects one bone to another and helps support a joint.

mobility—the ability to move about.

momentum—the tendency to keep growing or moving forward.

National Football Conference—one of the two conferences, or groups of teams, in the National Football League. The other group is called the American Football Conference (AFC). Both the AFC and NFC are further divided into four divisions, the North, South, East, and West Divisions.

renegotiate—discuss again a deal or an agreement with the hope of getting better terms.

sack—a play in which a defensive player tackles the quarterback behind the line of scrimmage.

scramble—to move quickly and with a sense of urgency.

vandal—a person who, out of the desire to cause harm, destroys public or private property.

Chapter 1

page 7 "It set the tempo . . ." Peter King, "Super Effort," *Sports Illustrated*, vol. 102, no. 4 (January 31, 2005), p. 42.

page 7 "I think . . . you've seen . . ." "Eagles Quotes: Game vs. Falcons: QB Donovan McNabb," Philadelphia-Eagles.com (January 23, 2005). http:www.philadelphiaeagles.com/news/eaglesQuotes.html

page 9 "I'm going to keep . . ." Mike Downey, "McNabb's Everything Not Enough," *Chicago Tribune* (February 7, 2005), p. S-1.

Chapter 2

page 12 "We told him we'd . . ." K.C. Johnson, "Definitely a Family Man—Syracuse, McNabb Bond Well," *Chicago Tribune* (December 26, 1996), p. S-3.

page 15 "It really started to . . ." Gerry Callahan, "Head Games," *Sports Illustrated*, v. 90, no. 20 (May 17, 1999), p. 38-41.

page 15 "When I was booed . . ." Don Pierson, "Boo Who? McNabb Shrugs Off Critics and Leads Surprising Eagles to 4-3 Start," *Chicago Tribune* (October 19, 2000), p. S-1.

Chapter 3

page 16 "Despite what happened . . ." Don Pierson, "McHigh Hopes: McNabb Finds Home in Philly," *Chicago Tribune* (August 4, 1999), p. S-1.

page 18 "We'll analyze . . ." Peter King, "Growing Pains," *Sports Illustrated* 93, no. 15 (October 16, 2000), p. 130.

page 21 "It was no big deal . . ." Michael Silver and Paul Zimmerman, "Back in Stride," *Sports Illustrated* 98, no. 2 (January 20, 2003), p. 44–45.

page 22 "I'm sure [Limbaugh's] not . . ." Donovan McNabb, quoted in "ESPN Analyst Resigns after Making Insensitive Comments about Donovan McNabb," *Jet*, 104, no. 17 (October 20, 2003), p. 50.

Chapter 4

page 28 "I wasn't tired . . ." "McNabb Fires Back at Critics and Controversy," PhiladelphiaEagles.com (April 29, 2005). http://www.philadelphiaeagles.com/news/Story.asp?story_id=4468

page 29 "On the field I'm . . ." Peter King, "Rock Steady," *Sports Illustrated*, v. 103, no. 12 (Sept. 26, 2005) p. 54.

page 30 "Terrell Owens has been. . ." Chris McPherson, "Owens Suspended, Team Reacts," PhiladelphiaEagles.com (November 5, 2005). http://www.philadelphiaeagles.com/news/Story.asp?story_id=6303

page 31 "Donovan doesn't have . . ." Nunyo DeMasio, "Where Is the Love?," *Sports Illustrated* 105, no. 20 (November 20, 2006), p. 60.

page 34 "Donovan has always done . . ." DeMasio, "Where Is the Love?," p. 62.

Chapter 5

page 38 "It was shocking . . ." "McNabb Addresses Draft, More," PhiladelphiaEagles.com (May 8, 2007). http://www.philadelphia-eagles.com/news/Story.asp?story_id=12527

page 39 "Donovan and I . . ." Larry Mayer, "Harris Apologizes to Grossman, Bears Teammates," ChicagoBears.com (June 18, 2007). http://www.chicago-bears.com/news/NewsStory.asp?story_id=3530

page 39 "I never said . ." Vaughn McClure, "McNabb: No QB Criticized Like Grossman; But Eagle Stands By His Race Statement," *Chicago Tribune* (September 20, 2007), p. S-7.

page 43 "It's always good . . ." "McNabb Rolling in His Strong Offseason," PhiladelphiaEagles.com (April 10, 2008). http://www.philadelphiaeagles.com/ news/Story.asp?story_id=15306

page 45 "We're working hard . . ." "McNabb Rolling in His Strong Offseason."

Numbers in ***bold italics*** refer to captions.

Numbers in **bold italics** refer to captions.

page

5: Jerry Lodriguss/Philadelphia Inquirer/KRT

6: Eric Mencher/Philadelphia Inquirer/KRT

9: Gary W. Green/Orlando Sentinel/MCT

11: Novartis/PRMS

13: NFL/SPCS

14: Syracuse University/SPCS

17: Gary Bogdon/Orlando Sentinel/MCT

19: Peter Tobia/Philadelphia Inquirer/KRT

20: B.L. Johnson/Philadelphia Inquirer/KRT

23: Campbell Soup Co./NMI

24: Ron Cortes/Dallas Morning News/MCT

27: Kirby Lee/NFL/SPCS

28: ESPN/NMI

31: MPR529/SPCS

33: Milk PEP/NMI

34: BGCP/PRMS

37: Philadelphia Inquirer/MCT

38: The Chronicle/KRT

41: Joshua Skaroff/SPCS

43: Booker Bienstock/SPCS

44: Kirby Lee/NFL/SPCS

46: Upper Deck/NMI

47: Food Network/Ferencomm/NMI

48: Roche Diagnostics/NMI

49: Michael P. Malarkey/WireImage

50: Campbell Soup Co./NMI

51: Newsweek/NMI

52: Tom Fox/Dallas Morning News/KRT

54: WCA/PRMS

Front cover: Hunter Marin/Getty Images
Front cover inset: Jerry Lodriguss/Philadelphia Inquirer/KRT

Michael Chatlien has been a freelance writer for the past ten years. During this time, he has written scripts for educational videos and chapters for social studies textbooks. In 2005, Michael wrote a feature length screenplay called *Overture* that won first prize at the Written Image Screenwriting Competition.